# Explore Science

Chris Maynard

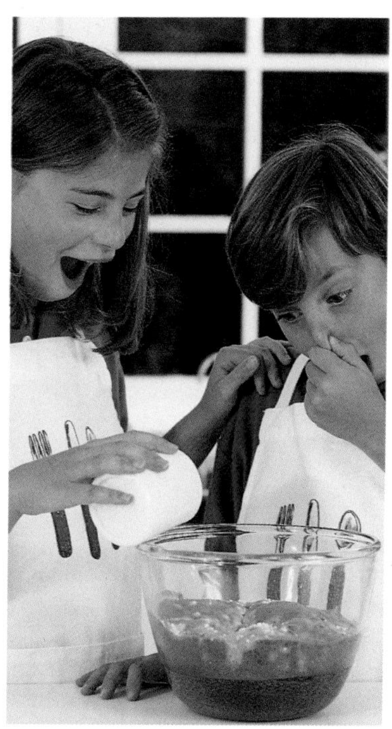

DK PUBLISHING

LONDON, NEW YORK, MUNICH,
MELBOURNE, and DELHI

**Senior Editor** Sue Leonard
**Senior Art Editor** Cheryl Telfer
**Publishing Manager** Mary Ling
**Managing Art Editor** Rachael Foster
**Photography** Steve Shott
**Jacket Designer** Chris Drew
**DTP Designer** Almudena Díaz
**Picture Research** Marie Osborn
**Production** Kate Oliver
**Science Educational Consultants**
Alison Porter and Frazer Swift
**The scientists** Olivia Forsey, Kathryn Foster, Rebecca Foster, Aaron Gupta, Elisha Hempsted, Alexander Khan, Hannah Leaman, Toby Leaman, and Peter Moggridge

First published as *Kitchen Science* in the United States in 2001
This edition published in the United States in 2011 by
DK Publishing
345 Hudson Street, New York, New York 10014

10 9 8 7 6 5 4 3
005-182185-Oct/2011

A catalog record for this book
is available from the Library of Congress.

ISBN 978-0-7566-8864-6

Printed and bound in China by Leo

Discover more at
**www.dk.com**

# Contents

To carry out the experiments in this book, you will need to find all the components from your home.

# Kitchen Lab

Here's some good news. Most kitchens make pretty good science labs. Take a look around yours. See if you can find any acetic acid, sodium chloride, and a liquid storage vessel or two.* If you can, then you're in business.

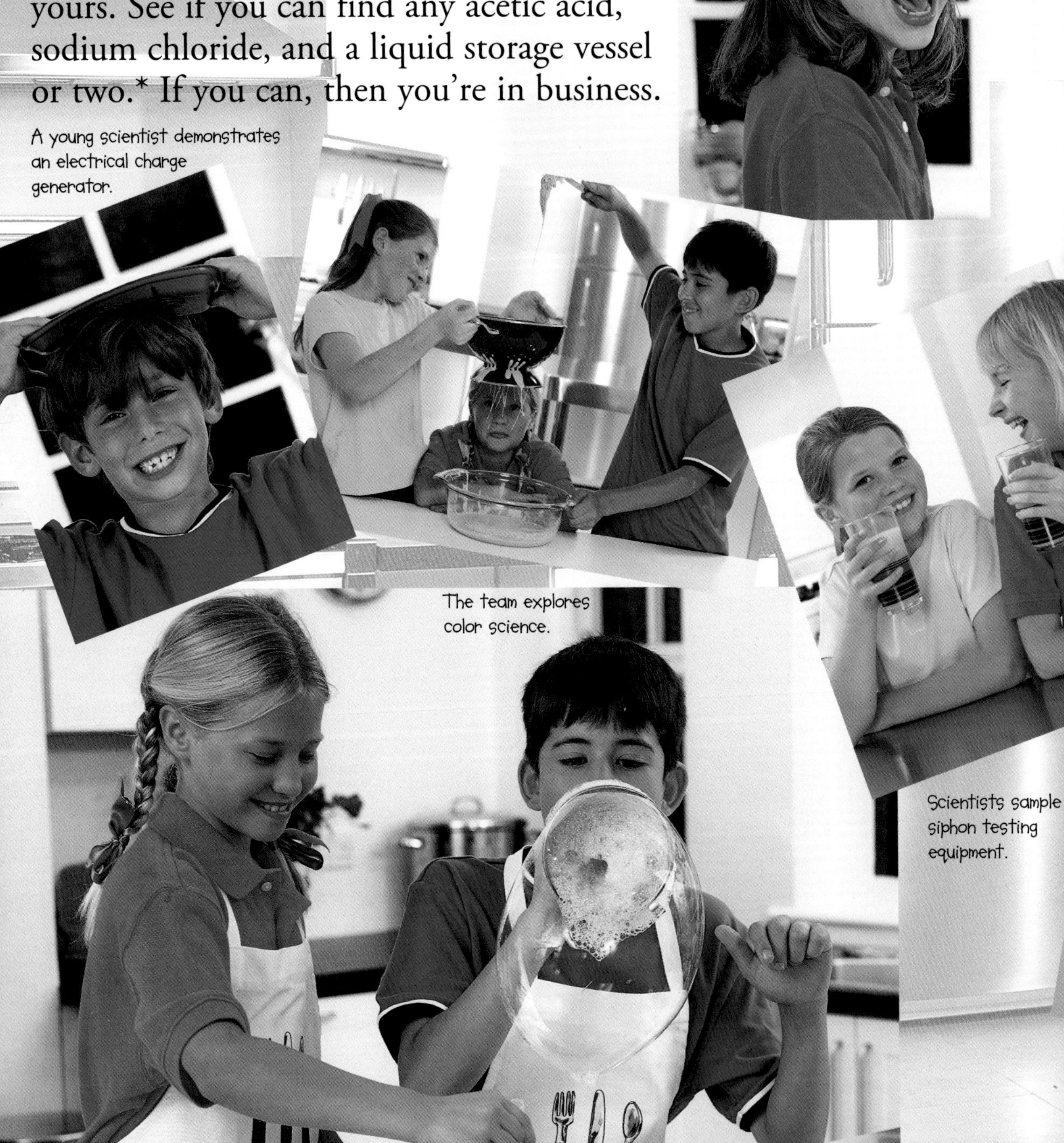

A young scientist demonstrates an electrical charge generator.

The team explores color science.

Scientists sample siphon testing equipment.

## Coming up

In the pages ahead you will find dozens of easy lab experiments to try out in your own kitchen. Some are smelly and some may get you wet or splattered with goo—though most won't. Science is a messy business?

### The science stuff

Now and then you'll come across a box like this. This is where you can find an explanation of the science in the experiment you just tried out.

Whenever you see this sign, it means take extra special care with the ingredients of your experiment.

This sign means that you ought to get an adult to help you do something that's a little trickier than usual.

Always check with an adult before you use any kitchen materials and equipment.

Keep a notebook handy to write down what happens when you do an experiment. You might stumble onto something that's really weird—or yucky.

*This is lab talk for vinegar, salt, and a plastic bowl.

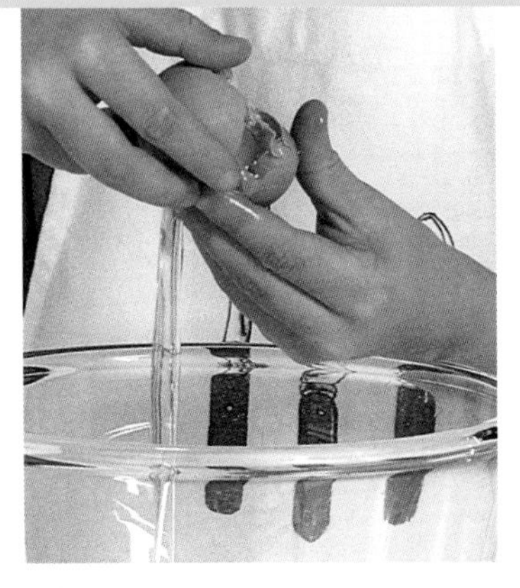

# Captain Cook

The yummiest thing about being in command of a kitchen lab is being able to snack on the results. Perhaps it's best to wait until after your friends have eaten before you tell them they've just swallowed an emulsion of albumen!

Break four eggs in half. Slide the yolk of each egg back and forth between the two half shells while you collect the runny egg white in the bowl beneath. You might need help!

## The white stuff

The cells of egg whites stretch like microscopic balloons when you beat them. They can hold so much air that a clear yellowish puddle of egg whites will swell to a thick white foam almost four times in volume. Add sugar and, hey presto, meringue mixture.

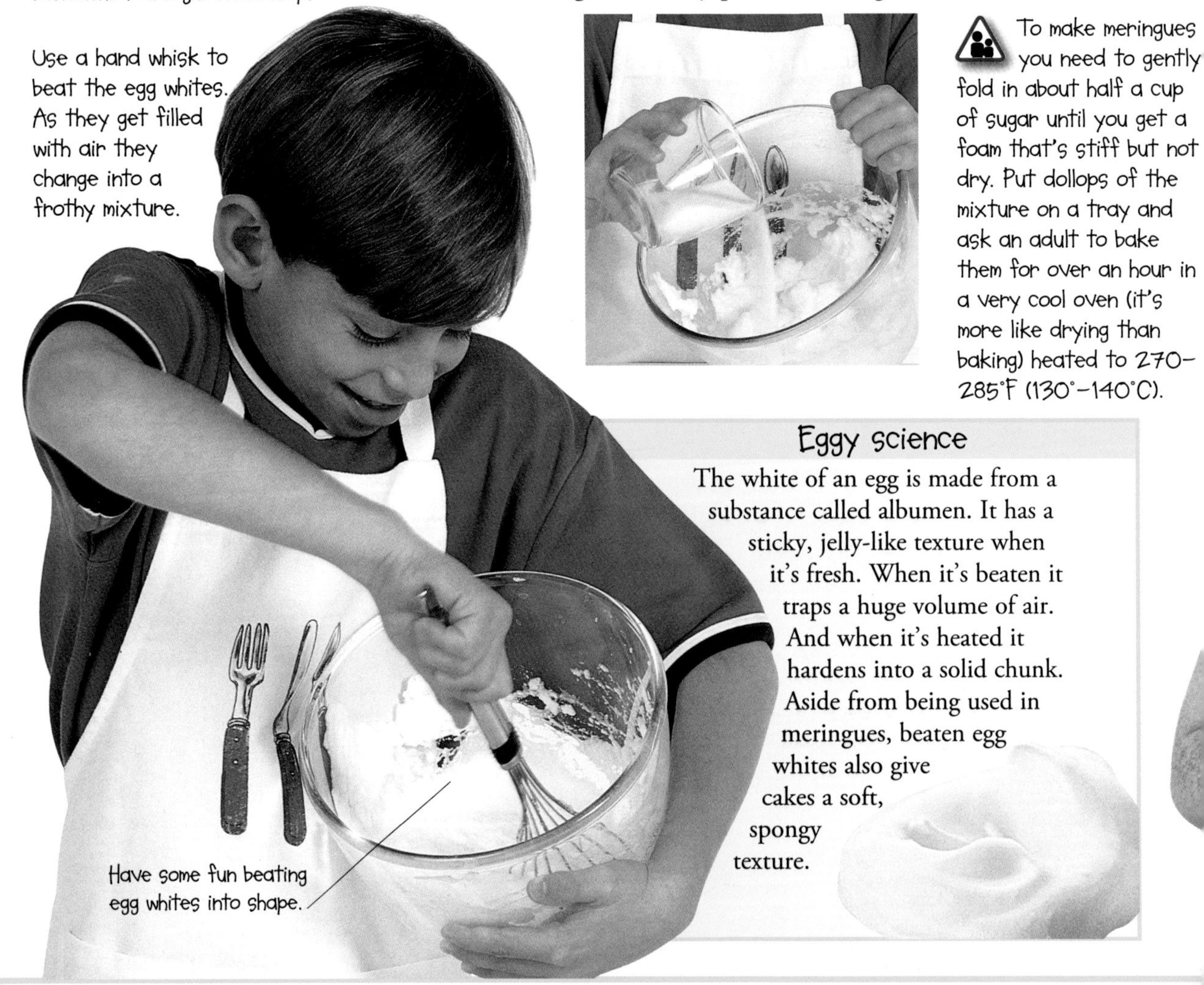

Use a hand whisk to beat the egg whites. As they get filled with air they change into a frothy mixture.

To make meringues you need to gently fold in about half a cup of sugar until you get a foam that's stiff but not dry. Put dollops of the mixture on a tray and ask an adult to bake them for over an hour in a very cool oven (it's more like drying than baking) heated to 270–285°F (130°–140°C).

Have some fun beating egg whites into shape.

### Eggy science

The white of an egg is made from a substance called albumen. It has a sticky, jelly-like texture when it's fresh. When it's beaten it traps a huge volume of air. And when it's heated it hardens into a solid chunk. Aside from being used in meringues, beaten egg whites also give cakes a soft, spongy texture.

## Butter fingers

In the days when people kept a cow, they often made butter by hand. Hardly anybody does it any more, yet it's not especially hard. Pour half a pint of whipping cream into a screw-top plastic container. Don't fill more than halfway. Add a pinch of salt. Put a heavy, squeaky-clean silver coin in with the cream.

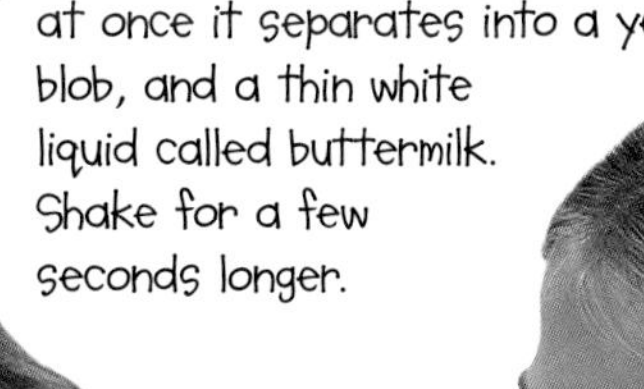

Screw the lid on tight. Shake like crazy for 15 minutes. At first the coin rattles freely and the cream sloshes about. Then thick whipped cream forms, and the sloshing stops. The whipped cream gets thicker. All at once it separates into a yellow blob, and a thin white liquid called buttermilk. Shake for a few seconds longer.

Pour off the buttermilk and spoon the yellow blob onto a cloth. Wrap it up and give it a good squeeze to get rid of the last drops of liquid. You've got pure butter. So... go and make toast!

### Buttery science

Most people think emulsion is a kind of paint. In truth, it's any mixture where tiny droplets of one liquid hang suspended in another. Like salad dressing—oil in vinegar. Or whipped cream—butterfat in water. As you churn whipped cream, you beat droplets of butterfat until they collapse and rejoin to form a single blob of butter.

# Manic Mixtures

An awful lot of mixing goes on in the kitchen, and normally you eat the results. But these strange concoctions are not for munching; they're for you to have fun with, and learn from, too!

## Nervous colors

Drive some innocent food colors absolutely crazy with this experiment. Get a dish of milk, let it warm to room temperature, and then dot drops of different food colors around it.

Dunk a toothpick into some dishwashing liquid and touch it in the center of the milk. The colors should head screaming to the sides of the dish. Dip the stick again but touch it to a blob of color this time and see what happens.

Use a drop of soap to ease the milk's tension

## Gruesome goo

This experiment works best with friends who don't mind getting gunky. Put two cups of cornstarch in a bowl and add food coloring. While one lab partner adds one cup of water—SLOWLY—the other mushes the mixture in the bowl by hand.

### Tense science

Look at a drop of water on a scrap of foil and see how a "sausage skin" of water holds it in shape. The "skin" is called surface tension. Soap rips surface tension apart. When soap touches the milk, the surface tension at that point snaps, but it is as strong as ever in the rest of the bowl. That's why the milk (and the colors) rush toward the side of the dish.

Get hold of some kitchen utensils and see how the goo works when you push it through holes or try to spoon it around.

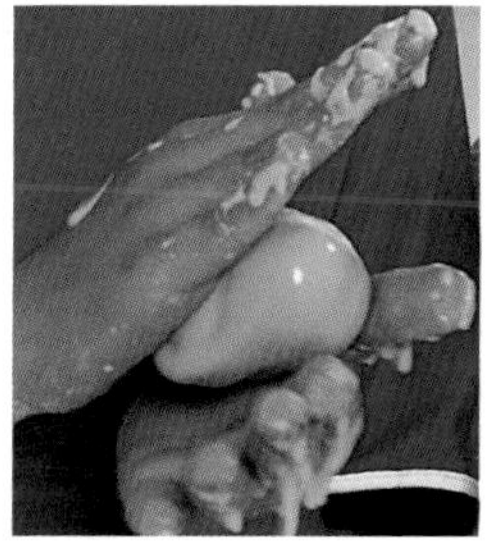

Roll it in your hands to make a solid ball. Stop and let the ball rest. It should slip through your fingers.

Squeeze a handful hard, then stop squeezing and open your hand.

Plunge your hands in and mess with your goo.

## Gooey science

Your goo is sometimes a solid and sometimes a liquid. That's because cornstarch doesn't really dissolve. It only forms tiny solid pieces that hang suspended in the water. Scientists call this strange type of liquid a colloid. The harder you press, the firmer they feel. But when you ease off and open your hand, they run and drip. The secret of handling colloids is this: slow for flow; hard for solid.

## Silly business

In the middle of World War II, an American engineer began to look for a cheap alternative to rubber. He made a goo that stretched and bounced better than rubber, but was much too soft and squishy to make into tires. One day, a toy shop owner saw someone playing with the goo. It looked like fun stuff, so he bought some, rolled it into balls, and sold them packed in plastic eggs. He called it Silly Putty®. Kids snapped up 750,000 sets in three days!

# Double Bubble Trouble

Mix half a cup of dishwashing liquid with a couple of pitchers of water in a large dish. The mixture will be better and stronger if you make it a day before you use it. Pull a metal coat hanger into a roundish shape. Plunge it into the mixture and pull it out slowly. Wobble the bubble around to make fun shapes.

You may not realize how much science there is in blowing a soap bubble. That's probably because your bubbles have been too small for any really good experiments. If so, just wait until you get you hands on these giants.

## Monster bubbles

Lots of people use little pots of bubble mixture to blow golf-ball-sized bubbles. But now it's time to think bigger. A LOT bigger. It's time to make some mega-bubbles longer than your arm and bigger than your head.

### Bubble science

When you blow air into a soapy film it swells like a balloon. Finally, it snaps shut and traps a puff of air inside itself to form a bubble. From being horribly stretched, the bubble now tries to relax to its original size. The air inside makes this impossible. So it forms the least stretchy shape it can—a ball. That's why all bubbles, no matter what they look like at first, end up sphere-shaped and not boxes, cones, or doughnuts.

## Color dome

Bubbles play wonderful tricks with light—just like rainbows. Here's an experiment to prove it.

Tape a flashlight to the bottom of a clear plastic lid. Hold it upright and spoon a little bubble mix onto the lid.

The flashlight shines up through the bubbles to create a rainbow-colored dome.

Stick a straw into the bubble mix and gently blow some bubbles to make a bubble dome. Step into a dark room and switch the flashlight on. Take a good look at the bubbles. What colors do you see swirling around? Do they ever change? What colors do you see just before a bubble pops?

A soap bubble skin is **500,000th of a centimeter** thick as it starts to pop

### Color science

All bubbles are a sandwich of soap and water. As they reflect light from a flashlight you can see the colors of the rainbow swirling on their walls. If you blow gently on a bubble, the colors change as the walls get thinner. When the bubble walls are at their thinnest the colors disappear, so just before a bubble pops, it appears to turn black.

Try dunking funnels or other kitchen utensils into the bubble mixture and blow air through them.

# Tower of Strength

The science of building is incredibly clever. Simply by changing the shape of your materials you can make them stronger, and by gluing small bricks together you can make one stable, solid object.

First build a tower out of plain sugar cubes. Stack one on top of the other and see how high you can pile them before they fall over.

## Sticky bricks

The secret of building structures that don't fall down is to use bricks AND cement. Try the recipe below to cement sugar cubes together in sixes. Then cement the sixes in layers. How high can this tower rise before it starts to wobble?

Tired of towers? Make an igloo with your sugar bricks.

Don't eat the cement! Raw eggs must be cooked before you eat them.

To make A-grade sugar cement mix three egg whites with one cup of icing sugar in a bowl, beat it into a thick paste, and slather it on. The thicker the cement the stronger the tower will be. Keep the mixture in an airtight jar so it won't dry out.

## Building bridges

It's obvious that a sheet of paper can't hold up a heavy load. Or can it? If you were an engineer you'd know a good few tricks for building strong paper bridges.

Tape a piece of card over the top of two tins to build a bridge. How many carrot slices can the card bridge hold before it collapses?

Try the different bridge shapes below and see which is the strongest. The corrugated bridge holds up a load well, because by pleating the paper you turn it into a set of upright lengths. Each upright has a lot more strength than a flat sheet. Together they make your bridge strong enough to take a huge load of carrot slices.

Keep piling on the carrots to see what shape makes the strongest bridge.

### Bridge science

A beam bridge is held up by pillars. The corrugated sheet makes a beam bridge, so does a girder. But an even stronger shape for bridges is an arch.

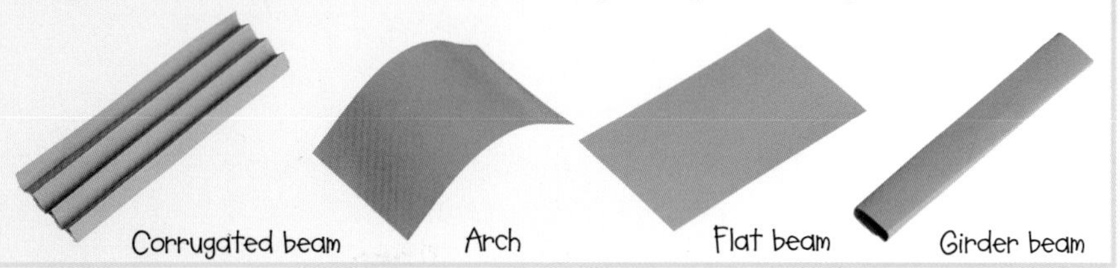

### Suspension bridges

These bridges use cables strung across tall towers to hold up heavy loads. The shape is so strong that it's the best way to span long distances. This picture shows the famous Golden Gate Bridge in San Francisco, USA, which is the fifth longest bridge in the world. The longest is the Akashi Kaikyo Bridge in Japan, which spans nearly 7,000 ft (about 2,000 m).

### Arch bridges

Arch bridges are one of the oldest types of bridges. They have an arc-shaped span in the middle. The arc carries weight along it's curve and out towards the two ends. This makes them stronger than a beam bridge because the two ends carry most of the load. Like this there's not much chance of the middle sagging.

# Moldy Stuff

If you already have warm feelings for mushrooms and fungi, then you'll really love molds. They all belong to the same family of plants but not one of them has any seeds. Instead, these plants grow from spores.

## Spore print

Mold, like mushrooms, grows from dust-sized specks. Take a spore print from a mushroom to get a good look at some spores, and to make an amazing pattern.

⚠ Find the biggest mushroom you can buy. Never use wild mushrooms, because they can be poisonous. Cut off the stalk. Set the mushroom face down on a piece of card, cover with a bowl, and leave it for a few days. The spores can range from white to black, so use a piece of card with a contrasting color.

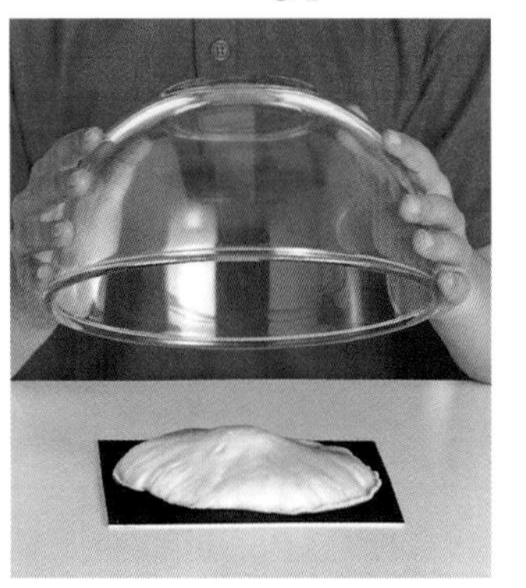

You'll be left with a pale, powdery ring when you take the bowl away and lift the mushroom up. These are the spores. Normally they blow away in the wind, settle somewhere damp, and start to grow into new mushrooms.

A fine sprinkling of mushroom spores.

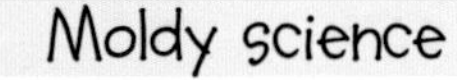

## Moldy science

Mold is a plant—a cousin of fungus. But instead of nice rich soil, mold prefers damp, rotting things to feast on. Mold grows as a tangle of threads. Inside are colonies of spore cases. Each case is a tiny pinhead with thousands of spores inside it. After the case breaks open, the spores sail away on the air looking for more moist food to land on and grow.

Moldy bread

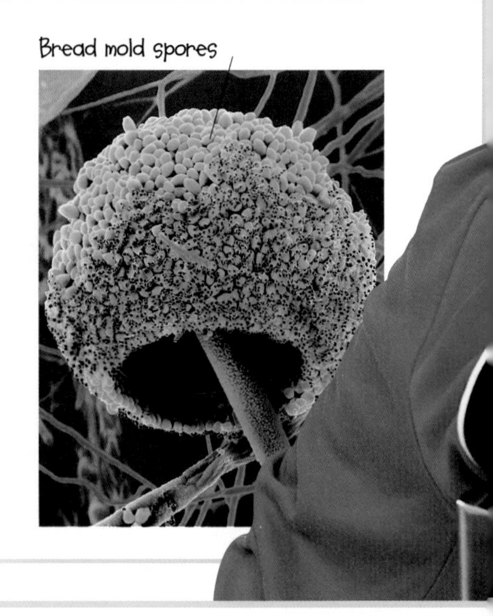

Bread mold spores

## Get moldy!

Want to set up a mold ranch experiment? You'll need chunks of leftover food like bread, cheese, vegetables, and fruit. Don't use meat or fish as they get highly stinky.

Dip the chunks in water. (Mold hates being dry.) Put them in a glass jar with a screw top and shut it tight. Tape the rim closed so nothing gets in or out.

## Thanks to a mold we get the life-saving drug called penicillin

Soon a fuzzy garden will start to grow. It's your mold crop.

After a few days you'll start to see patches of white, green, or blue growing on the food. They are mold. Which kinds of food got moldy first? Was the mold smooth or fuzzy? Did everything in the jar go moldy? Throw away the jar and the moldy remains when you're finished with them.

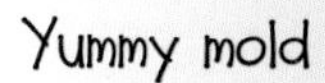

### Yummy mold

Mold belongs to the fungus family—just like mushrooms and mildew. It commonly grows on food, or the rotting remains of animals and plants. Most often we throw out food if it gets moldy. But when certain cheeses, like the ones with blue or green veins in them, get moldy they take on a delicious flavour. That's when we eat mold.

⚠ Special cheeses are fine to eat but mold isn't. Make sure you tape up the jars at the start of this experiment, and do not open them before you throw them away.

# Sour Power

Lemons are packed with sour-tasting juice. It is also a natural acid. This makes lemons the perfect things for all sorts of fruity scientific experiments.

## Lemon fizz

Most batteries are heavy tubes packed with chemicals. But other things can make electricity flow, too, and they don't look a bit like batteries. Take lemons, for example.

## Shocking science

What happened is that you created a natural battery. The science is the same as for man-made batteries. Lemon juice is a weak acid (that's why it has a sour taste). It reacts with the two different metals you stick into it to make an electric current. As long as a lemon has juice it has power.

⚠ Get a fresh lemon. Stick a short piece of copper wire into one side. Unbend a steel paper clip and plunge it into the lemon next to the copper wire. Now gently touch the free ends of the wire and paper-clip to your tongue. The tingle you feel is a current of pure electricity. Never use batteries or different wires for this experiment, as they could be dangerous.

## Lemon preserve

Mighty lemons can do a lot more than make electricity. They can also stop apples from turning brown. To start with, ask someone to cut an apple into quarters for you.

A lemon is a type of berry

Squeeze lemon juice onto two quarters. Leave one quarter with lemon juice and one without on the table. Put the other quarters in the fridge. Look at them a few hours later—the untreated slices will have gone brown.

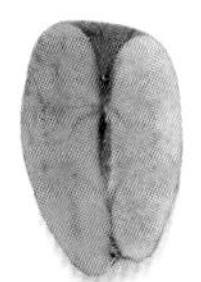

No juice/ no fridge

Juice/ no fridge

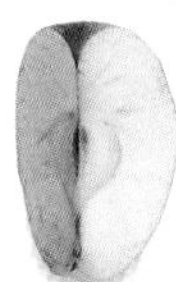

No Juice/ in fridge

Juice/ in fridge

## Discoloured science

When an apple is sliced the "cells" within it get ripped open. This means that the chemicals inside the cells can react with oxygen in the air, which turns the apple flesh brown. The acid in lemon juice (called citric acid) stops these chemicals in their tracks. Chilling the chemicals stops them too, which is why the apple quarters in the fridge don't get nearly so brown.

## Smells fishy

How do you keep a fish from smelling? Cut off its nose! How do you keep your hands from smelling after you handle fresh fish? Use lemon juice! Fishy scent comes from chemicals in the body oils of fish. It's hard to get rid of it with soap and water. But if you rub your hands with lemon juice, the acid changes the fish oil chemicals so that they rinse off under running water.

## Lemon float

Here's a way to show that lemons float—except when you peel them. Put a lemon in water, and watch it bob happily on the surface. Right now it is lighter than water.

Now pare the rind with a peeler. Back into the water it goes...and sinks. When you took off the rind you removed the lemon's life jacket, for the rind is full of thousands of tiny air bubbles. Take them away, and the flesh that's left is heavier than water.

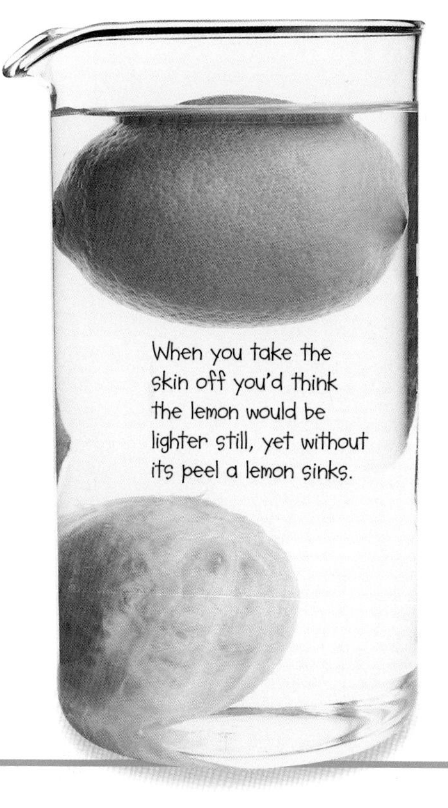

When you take the skin off you'd think the lemon would be lighter still, yet without its peel a lemon sinks.

Get some vinegar and add a little red food colouring to it. Use a funnel to half fill a small plastic bottle with baking soda. Now you are ready to create your own volcano.

# Fizzical Reactions

This is the sort of thing research chemists like to do—mix two different chemicals to cook up a third. In this case the chemist is you, and the new chemical you're going to make is a very common gas.

## Chemical eruptions

When we say "volcano" most people think of burning lava. But have you ever heard of a cold volcano? Well you have now, because with this experiment you end up making fizz not fire.

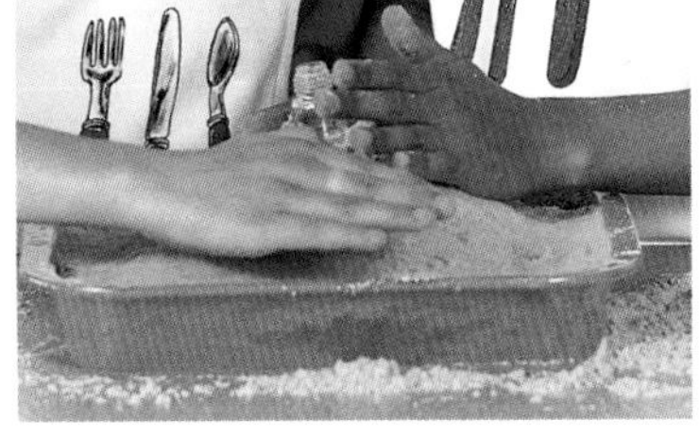

Put the bottle containing the baking soda in the middle of a large dish or tray. Pile sand around it to make a mini-mountain.

Pour the red vinegar mixture into the top of the volcano and prepare for a chemical reaction! If you get any of the "lava" on your skin, wash it off straight away.

## Inflated ideas

How can you use a liquid to inflate a balloon? Try this chemical concoction. It will leave you amazed, but not breathless. Stand back and watch the balloon blow up as if by magic.

Half fill a big bottle with a mixture that is half vinegar and half water.

Use a funnel to fill a balloon with baking soda. Then stretch the end of the balloon tightly over the top of the bottle.

Keep the top of the balloon dangling low until you are ready to inflate it. Then lift the balloon up so that the powder falls into the bottle. Now count the bubbles, thousands and thousands of them. And look what happens to the balloon.

### Gassy science

Why did the volcano erupt and the balloon expand? Because the soda (sodium bicarbonate) and vinegar (acetic acid) reacted and made a gas called carbon dioxide. A zillion bubbles of it were released, making both the lava flow and the balloon swell up.

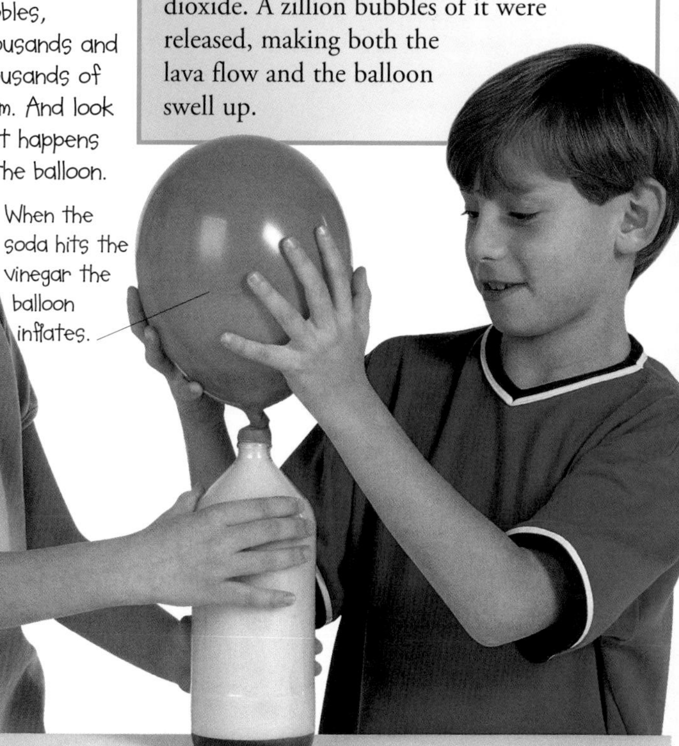

When the soda hits the vinegar the balloon inflates.

### Gas guzzlers

The gas you made in these experiments is the same carbon dioxide that fizzy drink makers put in their cans and bottles. In the factory, they bottle drinks at high pressure. The gas is squashed so hard that it all dissolves in the liquid.

When you open the top of a bottle, the pressure drops. There's a whoosh of gas and a cloud of bubbles starts to escape from within. They make your drink fizzy and taste good. They're also why you burp so loudly after guzzling a can of it. The scientist who invented fizzy drinks lived in Britain in the 1700s. His name was Joseph Priestly. He found that bubbling carbon dioxide through water gave it a bright and sparkling taste.

# Acid Tests

Suck on a lemon, or drip a drop of vinegar on your tongue. Why do they have that mouth-puckering taste? It's because both are weak acids, and all acids taste sour. Bases are the opposite of acids. Weak ones taste bitter and feel slightly soapy. Lots of washing powders are made with bases.

Get a jar of pickled cabbage and drain the red juice into a bowl.

## Crazy cauldron

This experiment mixes an acid and a base and gets some really fizzing and smelly results.

### Acid rain

When traffic and chimney fumes mix with rain, they may make it as acidic as lemon juice. The trouble with acid rain is that it reacts with much of what it touches, including buildings and trees.

⚠ Add baking soda to the bowl. The liquid will fizz and change color. Then add vinegar to the bowl. The liquid will fizz and change color again. The cabbage juice fizzes when you add the baking soda (a base) because pickled cabbage juice has vinegar in it—which is an acid

## Pink and blue

The easy way to tell acids and bases apart is with an indicator. It's a smart substance that can't be fooled. Plain red cabbage juice is an excellent indicator, but you'll have to get an adult to help you make it. It always changes to pink when it comes into contact with an acid and blue when it meets a base.

Ask an adult to chop up a head of red cabbage and put it to soak in hot water. After a few hours, drain off the reddish purple juice. Set up four jars of juice and rummage through the kitchen looking for acidic things to turn it pink and basic things to make it go blue.

Lemon juice is a weak acid, and so it turns the indicator red.

Distilled water isn't acid or a base. It's neutral, so the indicator doesn't change color.

Baking soda forms a weak base, so the indicator goes dark blue.

Milk of magnesia is a strong base, so the indicator goes green.

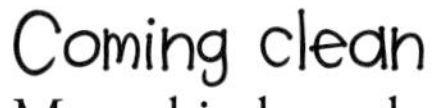

## Coming clean

Many kitchen cleaners are made from bases. This experiment uses baking soda, which works as a mild cleaner, and kitchen foil to bring a shine to silverware.

Put a cupful of baking soda in a bowl with six cups of boiling water. Get an adult to pour the boiling water in for you. Stir the mixture until the soda dissolves and add some strips of kitchen foil.

### Kitchen foil science

A bowl of kitchen foil and baking soda mixture creates an electric current—just like a car battery. It lifts the tarnish off the silver and deposits it onto the foil. As a result the silver comes out sparkling.

Put silverware in the mixture and in no time at all it should be sparkly clean. Rinse the silverware and give it a good polish. Then bask in the gratitude of your parents for polishing the silver (make sure you ask them first).

Use science to help you do kitchen chores

# Sinking Feeling

Do you think everyone in your class is dense? Well, they are, because everything has density, it's just that some things are more dense or less dense than others—just as these experiments show.

## On the level

Syrup, water, and oil all have different densities, and because less dense liquids always float on more dense ones, you can make your own density cocktail (not for drinking).

Pour syrup into a pitcher until it is about a quarter full. Then add the same amount of vegetable oil and the same amount of colored water.

### Dense science

If you weigh a piece of metal and a piece of cork that are the same size you will find that the metal weighs more. That means that the metal is more dense than the cork. That's why it sinks deeper in the pitcher than either the cork or the grape.

Use food coloring to color the water.

Syrup, water, and oil all have different densities and that's why they settle in these spectacular layers.

Is a cork more dense than oil? Where does the grape settle? Does the nut sink or swim?

The liquids separate into three layers, with the densest at the bottom and the least dense on top. Collect three objects—a metal nut, a cork, and a grape—drop them in and test which is most and least dense.

## Oily diving

A drop of oil is less dense than a drop of water. That's why it floats on top. Because oil and water don't mix well, there's a great diving trick you can play with them.

Take a large jar, and pour in some water about four fingers deep. Then add a finger or two of oil. When everything settles, which is the top layer?

Add a drop or two of food coloring. Does the color end up in the oil or in the water?

### Salty science

Salt is heavier than oil or water. It sinks as you sprinkle it on, and it carries a blob of oil down with it. The salt dissolves when it reaches the water. The oil is set free and at once floats back up to the top.

The oil hitches a ride with the salt and sinks down into the water.

Sprinkle salt on the surface. What happens next? You can make the oily diving last as long as you want just by adding more salt each time.

### Straw float

Pack a lump of modeling clay on the end of a drinking straw and you get a hydrometer (a tool that measures density). Put it in different liquids: water, oil, liquid soap, and see how well it floats. If the liquid is dense, it floats high. If not dense, it floats low. Which of your test liquids is the densest?

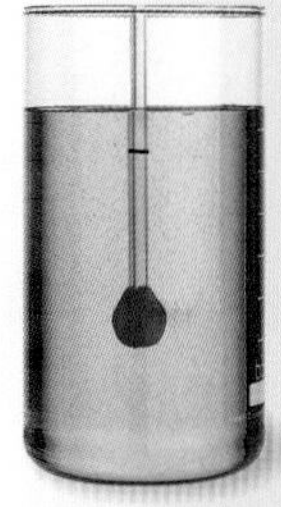

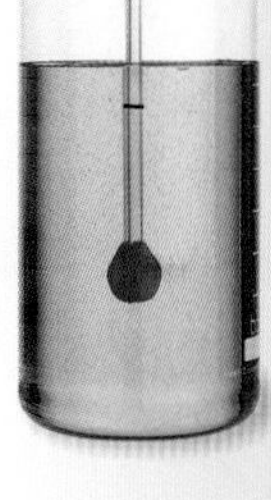

### Lava lamps

This weird invention was dreamed up by a man who knew that wax became less dense when heated. He took a tall jar, put colored wax at the bottom, filled it with liquid, and set it on top of a light bulb. The hot bulb melted the wax, and blobs of it rose up the jar. At the top they cooled, became denser, and sank—only to be warmed on the bottom and rise again.

# Chopping Mad

Scientists love the chemistry of food. Aside from helping them to discover the secrets of plants, it also allows them to nibble on some of their experiments if they ever need a snack.

## Sob story

Cut an onion and what happens? You burst into tears. But why? This experiment explains the whole blubbery mystery.

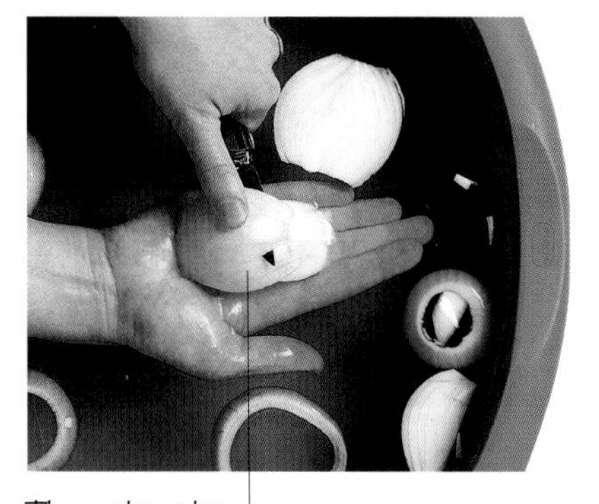

The water stops the onion "gas" from getting to you.

The next time an adult is preparing onions ask if you can help. First get them to peel an onion under water. Have a sniff around and you should stay dry-eyed. Then get them to chop onions up on a board and have a good smell. It will probably make you cry.

Don't touch the onions and then rub your eyes. It will only make things worse.

### Sobbing science

When an onion is cut open it let's out a strong gas that turns into sulphuric acid when it mixes with air. The acid is nasty stuff and stings like crazy when it hits your eyes. Under water though, the gas is largely washed away before it gets to you. Some onions are very mild. They grow in soil that makes them sweeter, and so they do not irritate the eyes at all.

## Slurping celery

We use knives and forks. Creatures use fangs and claws. But how do plants tuck into their food? The reason we can't see plants feeding is because it takes place in their roots and leaves. But with the right kind of experiment you can get an idea of what's going on.

Half fill a container with water and add a few drops of red food colouring. Stick celery in the water and leave it in a sunny place. The next day the celery will be reddish—which shows its sucked up water.

Tiny tubes in the stalk of the celery carry the water up to the leaves.

Central cylinder

Cortex

## Clever carrots

Aside from being a good source of vitamins and minerals, what's so special about carrots?

Get a grown-up to cut some slices and lengths of fresh carrot. Take a good look at the patterns of circles and lines. Do you know what they are?

## How celery feeds

From the sky, sunlight hits the leaves. From the air, carbon dioxide soaks into the leaves. From the jar, water mixes with both of them. A chemical in the leaves, called chlorophyll, makes food from sunlight, carbon dioxide, and water. In other words, celery isn't so much a hunter as a chef—it cooks up its own meals out of raw ingredients. The scientific word for this sort of food-making is "photosynthesis".

## Carrot science

Roots pull water and minerals from the ground. The part of the carrot plant that you eat is actually the root. The dark orange "central cylinder" of a carrot contains tubes that carry water up to the leaves, and other tubes that carry food back from the leaves to the tip of the root. The paler orange part of the carrot, the "cortex", is where the carrot stores food that it may need later.

# On the Move

Force is really important to scientists, and to everyone else, too. Without it no object could start or stop. See for yourself how the force of water can make things move, while the force of friction does everything it can to slow things down.

## Spinning wheel

Waterwheels are machines that use the force of flowing water to do hard work. In days of old waterwheels were built beside mills to turn heavy millstones and to grind grain into flour. They have a set of blades at their rim. Flowing water collides with the blades and forces the whole wheel to spin.

You can build a test waterwheel from two plastic plates. Make a hole through the centres of both. Make the holes big enough to slide the pencil right through to become the shaft of the wheel. Get six plastic lids from cans. Use strong glue or tape to attach them to the rim of one plate, all pointing the same way.

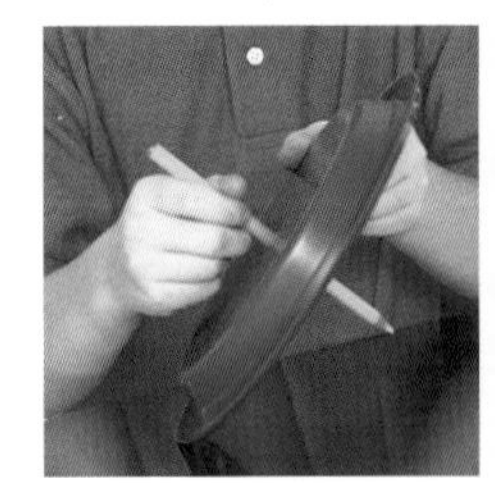

Space the lids out equally.

Glue the second plate onto the lids. The lids should be clamped together well. Now slide the pencil through the holes to make the axle of the wheel. Hold your waterwheel under running water.

Experiment by running the water slow and fast.

### Wheel science

Waterwheels are ancient inventions—over 2,000 years old. Their "engine" is flowing water. The faster it flows, the faster the wheel spins, and the more powerful it becomes. The axle carries this power to a heavy grinding stone within.

## Air power

A ball won't roll along the ground for ever. That's because there's a force, called friction, which slows moving things down. Anything that rubs on something else causes friction: the ground against the ball, a brake against a wheel, and so on. But there are ways to magic friction away.

The weight of a giant hovercraft can float as smoothly as a bottle top

For this experiment use scissors to cut the top off a plastic drink bottle. Make a very small hole in the bottle cap. You'll need something sharp to do this, so ask an adult to give you a hand. Then blow up a large balloon.

Pinch the neck of the balloon shut. Then carefully stretch the balloon mouth over the bottle cap (which is still screwed on tightly).

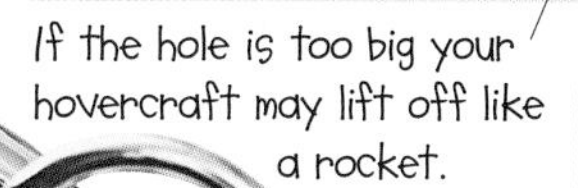

If the hole is too big your hovercraft may lift off like a rocket.

With the balloon in place, let go of the neck. As escaping air rushes out from under the rim of the bottle it creates a cushion of air. The bottle floats. Push it gently and see it glide across the table.

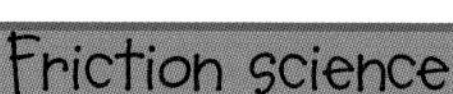

A cushion of air, like a film of oil, cuts the force of friction hugely.

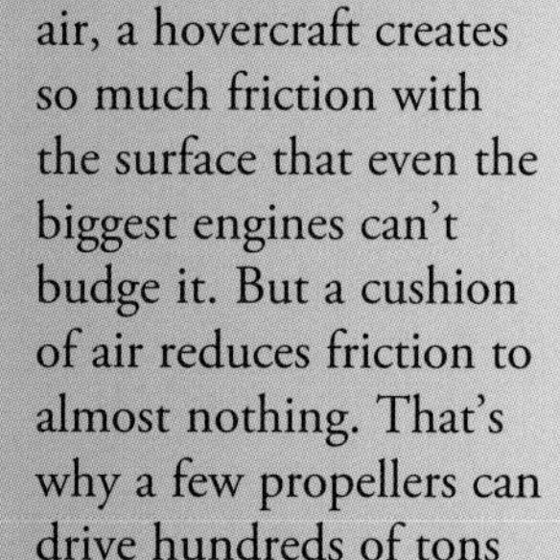

### Friction science

Without a cushion of air, a hovercraft creates so much friction with the surface that even the biggest engines can't budge it. But a cushion of air reduces friction to almost nothing. That's why a few propellers can drive hundreds of tons of machinery at high speed.

# Hot and Cold

A great law of science says that if you let hot things be, they cool down by themselves. But never, ever the other way around. Like water on a hill, heat can only flow downhill. Luckily, there's a delicious way to test this law.

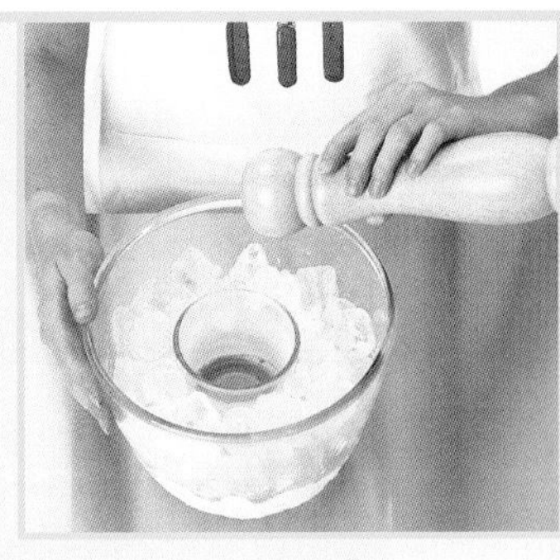

Mix a tablespoon of cream with two of milk and one of chocolate powder in a small glass. Put ice cubes in a bowl and sprinkle with salt. Put the glass on top and stack ice and salt around it.

## Salt freezer

Here's how to make ice cream the old-fashioned way!

Cover the bowl with a dish towel and leave it. Stir every few minutes.

After an hour, take the glass out of the bowl and taste some wonderful homemade chocolate ice cream. But how does it work? The towel stops warm air from flowing into the chilled bowl. Salt forces the ice to melt fast. The melting ice steals heat from the mixture, chilling it down until it freezes.

## Buttered peas

Heat flows like traffic—sometimes fast and sometimes slow. Some things, like copper, let heat flow through them quickly—they are good conductors—and some things make a complete hash of it. They are called insulators. Which is which in this experiment?

Get a wooden spoon, a plastic spoon, a metal spoon, and a straw. Use some butter to stick a pea at the same height on each item. Place them in a pot.

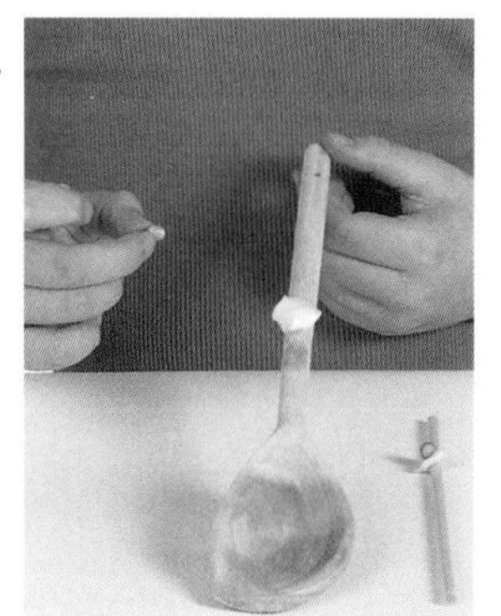

Pour some hot water into the pot. Which pea will fall first, do you think, and then in what order will the rest fall? Which is the best insulator? Which makes the best conductor?

### Conducting science

Every single thing in the universe is made up of tiny particles called atoms. If one end of a conductor heats up, the atoms inside it start to jiggle around like hot popcorn in a pan. They whack their neighbors and make these atoms jostle, too. Like this, heat shuffles along from atom to atom, until the whole conductor is hot. Metal is a good conductor, which is why it is used to make saucepans.

If you want to change the taste, try a drop of vanilla flavoring instead of chocolate.

The coldest it can ever be is about minus 459°F (273°C)

## Hot spot

If there's no place for heat to flow away, then whatever it's in stays hot. That's why a hot drink in a thermos flask stays hot all day. Here's how to test this.

Wrap and tape two layers of foil around a small jar (shiny side facing in). Pour warm water into the jar and screw on the lid.

Put a cork in the bottom of a big jar. Stand the small jar on it and screw on the lid. The water should stay warm because it's so hard for the heat to escape.

# Farming Crystals

Here's a useful law of nature: "If it isn't alive then it's probably a crystal." That's because just about every nonliving thing you can bump into is made of crystals, including rocks, metals, snowflakes, beaches, and even salt and sugar.

### Crystal science

All crystals have very regular shapes with flat surfaces and sharp edges. Many look like little boxes. It's all because their atoms are bolted together in orderly, geometric shapes. Usually you need a microscope to see them.

## Field of crystals

You need a watery solution to grow crystals. This one uses Epsom salts, because they make such wonderful spiked shapes.

Stir a tablespoon of Epsom salts into five tablespoons of warm water until it's all dissolved. Then gently pour the solution into a dark-colored shallow dish and place it in the sun.

As the water evaporates you'll see a crop of white crystal needles start to grow in the dish. They are Epsom salt crystals (or hydrated magnesium sulfate). Make sure you wash your hands when you finish.

## Grow a crystal

Growing crystals takes time. You won't need fertilizer, but you will have to "seed" crystals by growing them in a salty solution.

The small crystal acts as a seed. After a few weeks a much larger crystal grows around it as the water evaporates.

Make a salty solution by dissolving as much salt as you can in a jar of warm water. Pour a little of the solution into a shallow dish. Let it evaporate for a week. Then pick out the biggest crystal and tie yarn to it. Dangle the crystal from a pencil into the jar of solution.

## Crystal icicles

Over thousands of years, dripping water leaves great columns of minerals in caves. Those that cling tightly to the roof are called "stalactites." But if they sit, mightily, on the cave floor then they're called "stalagmites." Here's how to grow a crystal icicle—a stalactite—without having to go caving or wait 1,000 years. This one takes about a week to grow.

### Stalactite science

Water dissolves limestone as it seeps through the ground. As it drips from the roof of a cave it leaves behind a thin crust of limestone minerals. Slowly, very slowly, the crust grows into a long stalactite.

Fill two jars with warm water. Add baking soda and stir until you can't dissolve any more.

Take a length of thick yarn and attach a paper clip to each end. Lower the ends of the yarn into a jar so that it is suspended between the two. Place a dish under the lowest part of the yarn to catch the drips. Let the experiment sit for several days.

Quartz is the **most common** crystal of all

The solution of baking soda soaks the yarn and when it gets to the lowest point of the yarn it drips. Each drip leaves a little soda behind. Drip by drip, the soda crystals grow. After a few days, you'll have a white stalactite hanging from the yarn.

You might even get a stalagmite growing up from the dish.

# Wet, Wet, Wet

Water is pretty important in the kitchen, but have you ever thought about the changes it goes through every day? Heat it up or cool it down, and some rather weird things start to happen.

## Light at the top

Did you know warm water is lighter than cold water? So if hot water weighs a tiny bit less than cold, does it float on top? You may get soaked with this experiment, but at least you'll get an answer.

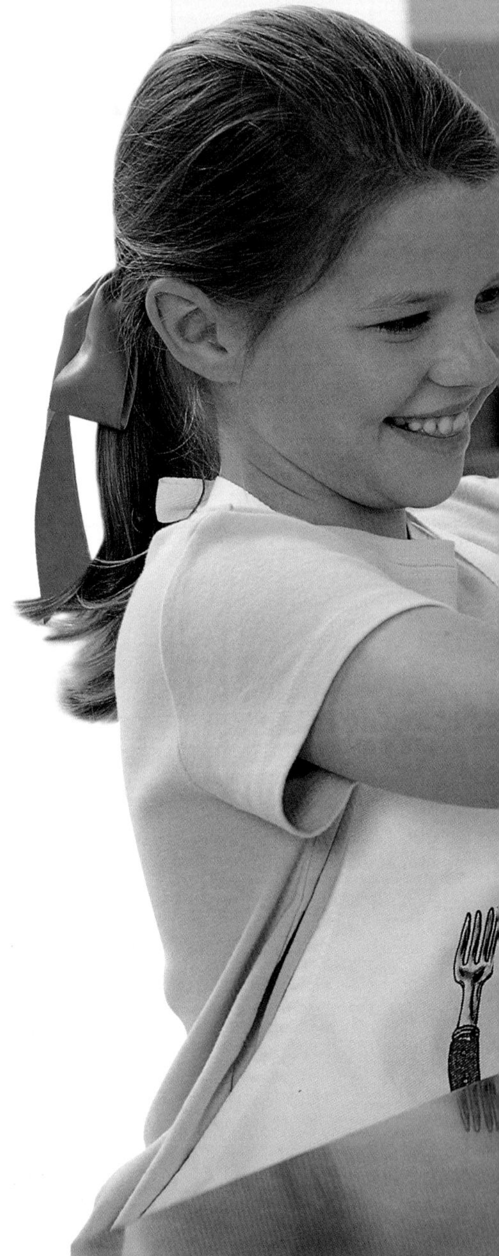

## Makes a change

For this experiment you hardly have to do a thing, just hang around the kitchen and you'll see how water goes through some pretty amazing transformations.

Heat up water enough and it turns into a gas called steam. The steam escapes into the air where it mixes with clouds and other moisture.

Steam

Watch the drips of a leaky tap. This is the liquid state in which we see water most often, although it only looks like this between a temperature of 32°F (0°C) and 212°F (100°C).

Water

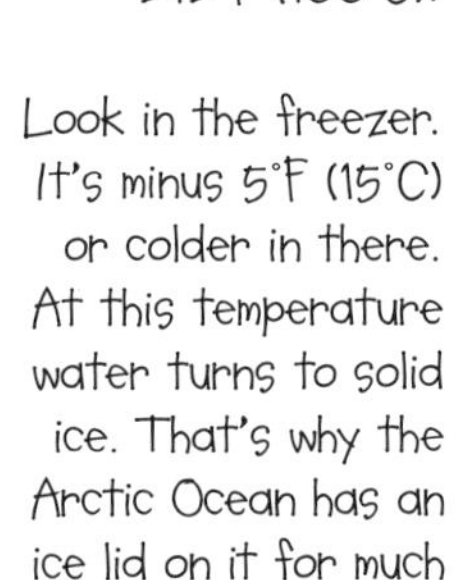

Look in the freezer. It's minus 5°F (15°C) or colder in there. At this temperature water turns to solid ice. That's why the Arctic Ocean has an ice lid on it for much of the year.

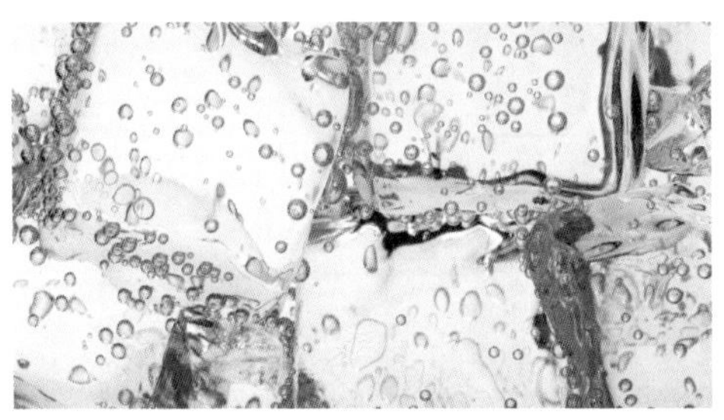

Ice

Find two jars exactly the same size. Fill one with hot water and add a drop of red food coloring. Fill the other with cold water and add blue food coloring. Fill up the jars until the water bulges over the rim.

## Watery science

Hot water is less dense than cold water, so it floats on top of it. That's because less dense things float on more dense ones. Lighter warm water always rises to the top of cold dense water. This is especially important in the sea since it helps currents to flow around the world.

Gently place a square piece of cardboard over the red jar so it seals in the water. Now you have to act quickly. Pick up the red jar and flip it upside down. If you get it right, the water will hold the cardboard in place. If you don't—you'll get soaked.

You may have to practise flipping the top jar a few times.

Put the red jar exactly on top of the blue jar. Hold them together and get someone to ease the card out carefully. What happens? Try the same experiment, but with the blue jar on top. What happens to the colours this time?

Fill a pitcher with juice and dip the end of a clean tube into it. Suck on the other end of the tube until juice nears your lips. Then quickly cap the tube with your thumb.

# Under Pressure

Nothing makes water happier than when it's flowing downhill. All it needs is a clear channel and enough pressure to send it on its way. From then on it just flows until it reaches the lowest level it can find.

## Juicy siphon

A siphon is a pump that runs on natural pressure and nothing else. That's why it can only flow one way—from a higher level to a lower one.

### Siphon science

As liquid flows down the long side of a siphon, it draws up more on the short side. If the long side ends lower down than the short side, the liquid keeps on flowing. Siphons have a gentle sucking action—this is why they are used in toilet cisterns and to drain gas tanks.

Once you get the juice flowing it won't want to stop.

Put the capped end of the tube in a glass and take your finger away. Juice will flow up out of the pitcher and into the glass. Keep the pitcher higher so the juice always runs downhill.

Move from glass to glass so each gets a fair share of juice.

## Fountain attack

With this science trick, offer victims a drink of water (even though it will never end up in their mouths). Fill a plastic bottle right to the top with water. Put the cap on tightly. Lay the bottle on its side and make a small hole about halfway down with a pen.

f you are feeling extra vicked, get your victim to nake the hole without telling im why.

Hold the bottle with the hole pointing at your victim. Ask if he wants a drink of water. Water won't flow out of the hole while the cap is on because no air can get in at the top. Then unscrew the cap and watch as a jet of water shoots out.

The lower the hole in the bottle, the more water pressure there is above it and the farther the fountain will splash.

## Nell, blow me down!

Jse an old law of science to trick your riends. Bet them that you can lift a ball ıp simply by blowing on it. They'll ıever believe you can do it, until they ee it with their own eyes.

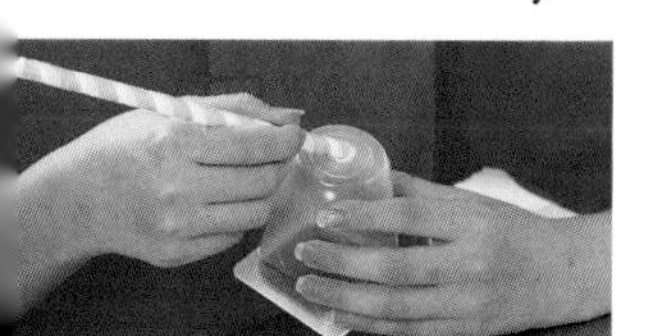

Take a small yogurt cup and nake a hole in the bottom. eed a straw through and seal t in place with modeling clay.

### Blowing science

What happens is this: As air speeds up its pressure drops so much that nearby air rushes in to fill the gap. When you blow, in-rushing air tries desperately to get up into the pot. The ball is in the way of the air, so it gets pushed up into the pot—even though you are still blowing with all your might.

Place the cup over a ping-pong ball and blow hard (don't suck). The ball will rise into the cup and spin as if you were sucking as hard as a vacuum cleaner.

# Creating Currents

Why are thunderstorms like combing your hair? Because both can create lightning. The kind on your head is just a crackle, but the bolts that zap between clouds are five times hotter than the surface of the sun.

## Hairy lightning

This experiment makes one of the tiniest bolts of lightning you'll ever see. It's an example of static electricity—the kind of charge that happens when two things rub together.

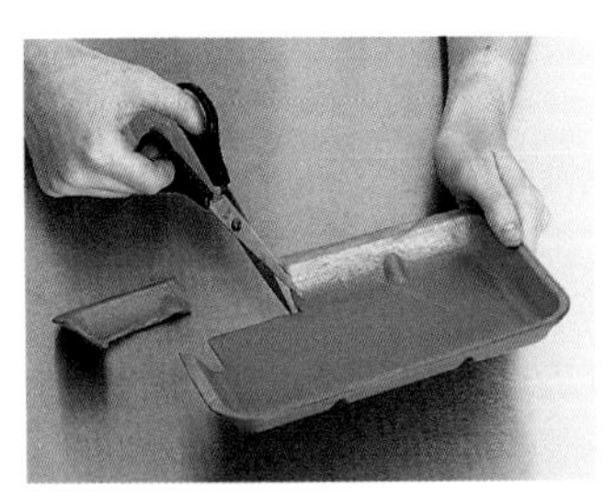

Cut a piece from a Styrofoam tray so that you end up with a bent corner.

Lightning makes a supersonic shock wave that we call thunder

Tape the bent section to the center of an aluminum pie pan to form a handle. Now rub the rest of the tray quickly across your hair.

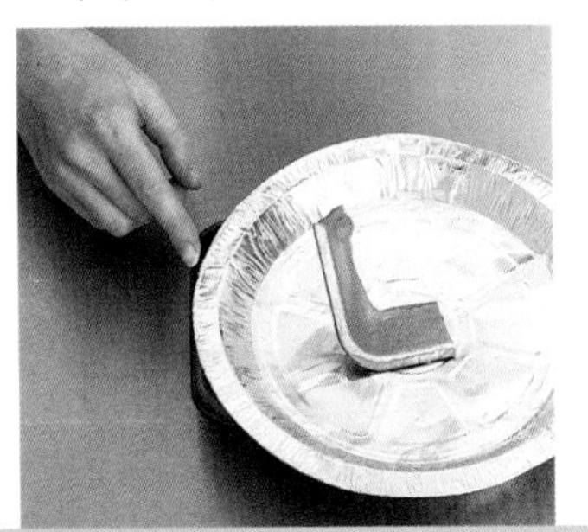

Set the tray upside down on a table. Using the handle ONLY, pick up the pan, and drop it onto the tray. Very slowly touch the pan with the tip of a finger. Watch how a spark flies! Do this in the dark if you want to see colored lightning.

### Sparky science

Rubbing the tray on your hair piles up an electric charge on it. The pan pulls some of the charge off the tray. As you touch it, the charge surges toward you as a spark. When the same kind of thing happens in clouds it creates lightning.

Sprinkle a bit of salt and pepper onto a plate. Now rub a pen very hard with a woolen cloth so it collects a charge. Wave the pen slowly over the plate, and the pepper jumps up and sticks to it. The salt stays behind.

## Pepper un-shaker

You can separate salt from fine-ground pepper two ways: very slowly with your fingers, or quickly by letting static electricity do the hard work. The trick is that pepper weighs a lot less than salt.

Both pepper and salt are attracted. But because the pepper is lighter it leaps up first. If you lower the pen too much you'll get the salt sticking, too.

## Water power

Not even water can resist the charms of electricity. With this experiment you can use static electricity to bend water flowing from a faucet.

Rub a balloon hard on your hair. Then hold it close to a thin stream of flowing water. The flow bends as it is attracted by the static in the balloon. How attractive are you? Rub a few balloons on your hair and then stick them to yourself to find out.

## Attractive Greeks

Static electricity was first investigated in ancient Greece about 2,600 years ago. A Greek philosopher named Thales found that when he rubbed amber (a honey-colored fossilized resin) with cloth he could attract pieces of straw to it. The Greeks called amber *elektron* and from it we get our word *electricity.*

## Striking lightning

A bolt of lightning is created when water droplets and ice crystals in clouds are whirled together so hard they become charged with static electricity. Opposite charges collect at the top and bottom of a cloud until the attraction between them is so great that a bolt of lightning leaps between the two (like the spark from your finger to the pan).

# Hard and Soft

Think of something hard? No, not maths—just something that's hard when you touch it. Now guess what happens if you heat it or freeze it? Many things go through near-magical changes if we play around with their temperature.

Put your piece of the chocolate in the fridge.

## Melting science

Everything goes soupy if you heat it enough. This temperature is called its melting point. For example ice melts at 32°F (0°C), and lead melts at 622°F (328°C). But you have to heat iron up to 2,802°F (1,539°C) before it melts.

## Getting warmer

Play a chocolatey trick on a friend. Put a slab of chocolate in the fridge overnight. Leave another piece somewhere warm. Next day put the two pieces out ready to be eaten. Pick up your rock hard piece and have a bite. It may be almost impossible to take a nibble. Then offer the other piece to your friend. But be careful, things might get a bit sticky.

It may have melted, but it's still chocolate!

Cold chocolate is so hard it clanks against the plate.

## Getting harder

Pick up a piece of bread and feel how soft and squeezy it is. Now put a couple of slices in the toaster and let them cook. Once they pop up, and cool, what do you notice first? Of course—toast is harder and crunchier than untoasted bread and a lot drier too.

Toast is just a nice sounding word for slightly burned bread. As bread roasts it forms a layer of ash (the brown and black specks) just the same as wood and paper do in a fire. Meanwhile, the moisture that made the bread soft evaporates to leave a warm toasty texture that's delicious with butter and honey.

Heat makes some things **go harder and others go softer**

## Getting solid

A fresh egg is runny and sloppy. But after boiling it in water (get help with this) for a few minutes the white goes hard. The yolk stays runny. Boil it a little longer and the yolk hardens too. So heat sometimes makes things go from liquid to solid.

## Getting wetter

Hold an ice cube in your hands for a few minutes. It starts out dry, but soon it gets very wet. That's because ice goes from solid to liquid as it gets warmer.

## Toasty science

When a slice of bread is toasted, it starts to burn. Burning is a chemical reaction during which oxygen in the air reacts with chemicals in the bread to give off heat and smoke, and to leave behind dark black ash.

## Juice, rocks, air

Apple juice is liquid, rocks are solid, and air is gassy. In fact every single substance in the world is one of these three: a gas, a liquid, or a solid. This trio is also called "The Three States of Matter".

Under the right conditions, apple juice can turn into a solid or a gas. Stick some in the freezer overnight and it will be in a rock hard state by morning. Boil it up in a pot and it will turn into a gas (steam) and evaporate into the air.

Any substance you name can change from one state to another. Solid rock will turn into a liquid if you heat it enough. Just visit an active volcano to see rocks flowing like honey. And if you take a bottle of air and chill it in outer space you'd see it turn into an icy liquid.

# Light Fantastic

Light is pretty useful stuff. Without it, you couldn't read the words on this page or see the faces of your friends. When you bend light it can make things look bigger, and sometimes it splits into different colors to make a rainbow.

## Color detective

Many colors are not true colors. Instead, they are mixed from other colors. Here's an experiment that sorts out the true from the mixed.

Get candy-covered chocolates and pick out different colors. Put a few of each color in a saucer and add water. Turn them so that the color comes off and mixes with the water. Cut coffee filters into strips, and put one in each of the saucers. As the colors move up the filters, the mixed ones separate.

### Color science

Light comes in waves of different lengths and our eyes see each length as a color. The shortest waves that we can detect are violet. After that they lengthen into blue and green, then yellow and red. The longest visible light waves are a deep-red color.

## Gelatin glasses

Did you know you can make a magnifying glass out of a dessert? It's not hard—especially if you like the taste of Jell-O.

Take a large pack of gelatin dessert. Lemon or any pale color works best. Get a grown-up to boil 1 cup (200 ml) of water and to put it in a pitcher. Dump the "raw" gelatin into the bowl and carefully pour the water onto it. Stir until the gelatin has dissolved.

After the mixture cools, put some in a ladle. You can also use a soup spoon or large measuring spoon. Carefully set the spoon on a dish. Put it in the refrigerator.

Four hours later the gelatin should be set. Turn the spoon out onto a wet, clear plate. If you are using smaller spoons you can turn them out onto some clear plastic, like a cassette-case lid. Run hot water over the back of the spoon to free the sticky gelatin.

## Magnifying science

The gelatin mold forms a curved lens that bends light rays—just like a magnifying glass. Light rays pass through it and spread out. They form an image that appears to be bigger than the words or pictures you were originally looking at.

Glasses were **first worn 700 years** ago in Europe

Hold the gelatin blob over words or pictures, and you'll have a lens that magnifies them. Two small blobs of Jell-O give you gelatin glasses!

The curved surface of the Jell-O makes beams of light bend so that they magnify things.

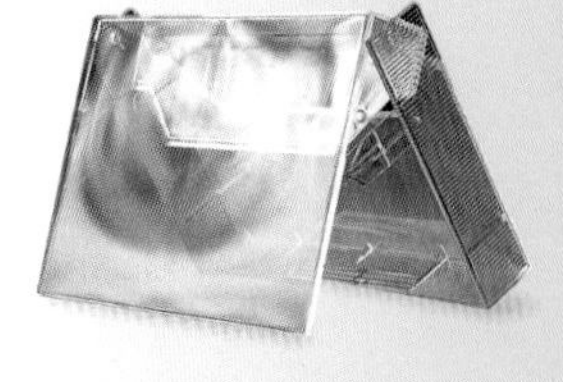

## Fake rainbow

You can make colors appear in clear plastic, but you'll need a pair of polarized sunglasses. Shine a bright light at a cassette box and then look at it through a pair of sunglasses. You should see a rainbow effect made up of bright colors. The polarized sunglasses cut out some of the colors that make up white light, and you see the colors that are left.

## Rainbow science

Real rainbows happen after clouds start to clear and sunlight strikes raindrops that are still falling. The light bends and travels onward to your eye, so you see it split into many colors.

# Making Sense

Human beings have five senses: smell, taste, sight, hearing, and touch. Smell and taste are really important because without them there would be no point in having fantastic inventions like pizza and ice cream!

Half-fill four egg cups with water. Squeeze the juice from half a lemon into one, add two teaspoons of sugar to the next, two teaspoons of salt to the third, and a little tonic water to the last one.

## Tongue map

The surface of your tongue is covered in hundreds of tiny taste buds. Here's an experiment that will show you just what your tongue can do.

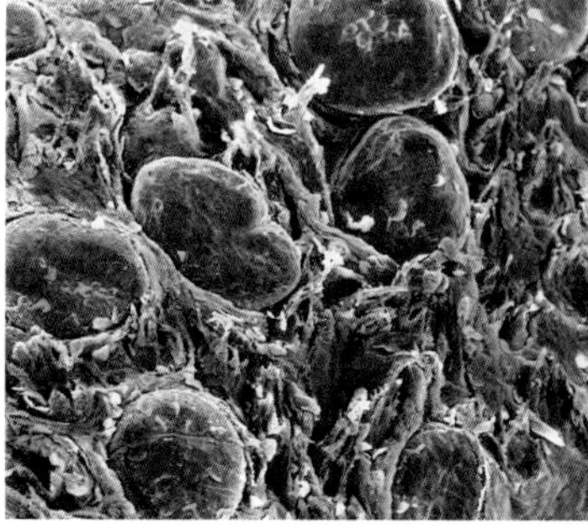

You may think that you taste with your tongue, but it only does a small part of the job—it gives you a rough idea of what kind of taste (like salty or sweet) you get from a particular food or drink.

Dab your tongue with paper towel before you taste from each egg cup.

Use a cotton swab to try each mixture. Touch it to the middle, sides, and back of your tongue. Which parts of your tongue are best at sensing salty, sweet, sour, and bitter flavors?

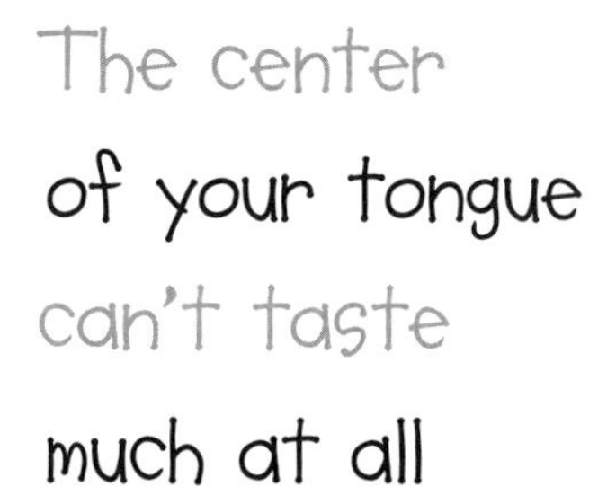

The center of your tongue can't taste much at all

## Blind tasting

When it comes to tasting—identifying individual flavours—your nose much is more important than your tongue. That's why, when your nose is blocked up with a cold, food loses its flavour. Try this test to prove it.

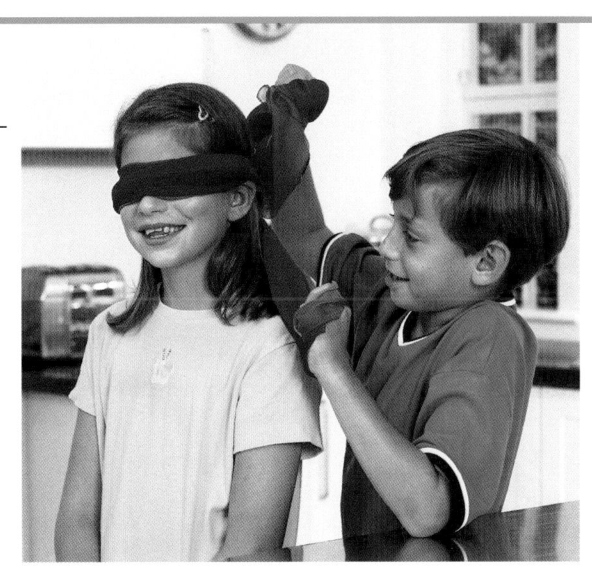

1. Pour three different fruit juices into three glasses. Get a friend to blindfold you with a scarf and then taste each glass.

Rinse your mouth out with water between tastings so it doesn't get too confused.

2. Now pinch your nose shut and do it again. How hard is it to tell one juice from another? Nose open—it's easy to tell one fruit flavor from another. Nose shut—smell turned off—and the juices all have the same dull flavor.

### Tasty science

Although you can identify hundreds of kinds of food, your tongue only knows about five tastes: sweet, sour, salty, bitter, or umami (savory). These can be picked up all over your tongue.

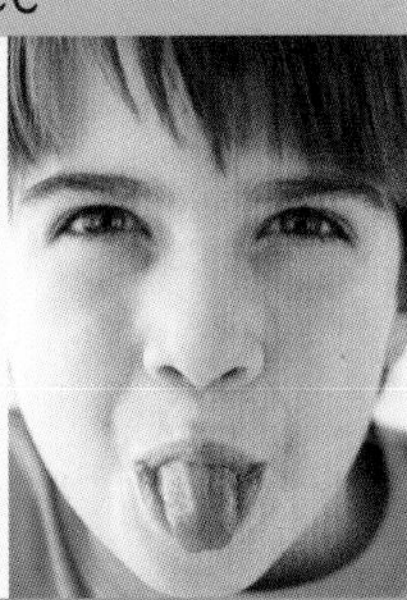

### Smelly science

We smell things at the very top of our nose, where there are two postage-stamp-sized patches of about 10 million "smell" cells. When a smell bumps into these cells they send a message to the brain, which has an excellent memory for sorting smells.

### Get touchy

Can you rely on your sense of touch to let you know when things are hot and cold? Try this experiment to find out. Get three glasses and fill one with hot water. Fill another with cold water and ice. Put a mixture of hot and cold water in the third glass. Put one finger in the hot water and another in the cold. Leave them for a minute.

Dip the hot finger into the warm water. The warm water will feel cold because it's not as hot as your finger. Try dipping the cold finger into the warm water. The water should feel hot. This is because you can only feel if something is hotter or colder than your skin.

# Seeing Sound

Sounds actually make things move, and although you can't see sound, you *can* see how it works. These experiments show that there really are sound waves bouncing through the air.

## Sound-wave science

The tin keeps vibrating after you hit it. As it vibrates, so does the air around it, and these small vibrations, called sound waves, spread out in all directions. When they reach the tin drum, they start it vibrating, too, and make the sugar jump up and down. Some of the sound waves also hit the drums in your ears (your "eardrums") and when they vibrate, your brain interprets this as sound.

Sound waves go through air and make the skin vibrate.

As you whack the sheet, it vibrates, creating sound waves

Cut along the side and bottom of a plastic bag that's big enough (when it's opened flat) to cover an empty cookie tin. Stretch it tightly over the tin to form a "skin" and anchor it with a rubber band. Pour on a little brown sugar. Hold a baking sheet near the tin and bang it with a spoon. What happens to the sugar?

Sounds are made when something vibrates—sometimes you see the vibrations, sometimes you don't. When these kettle drums are bashed, the skins move, sending out huge sound waves.

The sugar on the skin jiggles up and down—dancing in time to the music.

## Air gun

Here's how to make an air gun that can blow out a candle. The "bullets" it fires are blasts of sound.

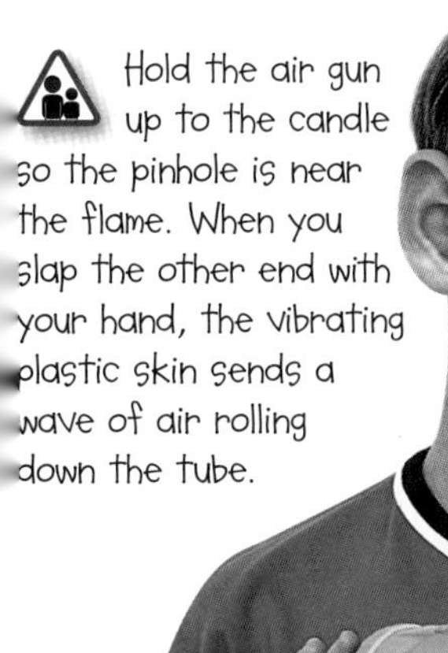

Set a candle on a dish and fix it in place with modeling clay to stop it from wobbling. Even a little cake candle will do. Ask an adult to light it.

Cut out two circles from a plastic bag. With a pencil, make a hole in the middle of one of them. Slip them over the ends of a cardboard tube and pull them very tight using rubber bands—if you need to, use tape to make them even tighter.

Hold the air gun up to the candle so the pinhole is near the flame. When you slap the other end with your hand, the vibrating plastic skin sends a wave of air rolling down the tube.

When the wave hits the small hole, it shoots out hard enough to blow out the candle.

## Sounds powerful

If sound waves can blow out candles and make sugar dance, what else can they do? Loud sounds can make a teetering bank of snow slide down a mountain to form an avalanche. And oil explorers explode dynamite to bounce sound waves off underground rock. Studying the echoes tells them where to find pools of oil.

## Fast sounds

The roar of jet engines is so loud, it deafens airport workers unless they wear earmuffs. Sound travels through air at about 1,115 ft (340 m) a second (a bit faster than most jets). In seawater, it goes five times faster still! Warships send sound waves (sonar) into the sea to find submarines.

# Hearing Waves

You hear sound when sound waves hit your ears. These waves are made when something vibrates (moves fast), and the air around it moves, too.

Using a sharp pen or pencil, poke a small hole in the bottom of two plastic cups (yogurt cups are fine). Be careful!

## Earphones

Sound waves can travel through solids, too. So, use a length of string and two plastic cups to make a simple phone that you can use to trade secrets with a friend.

Take a 15 ft (5 m) length of string. Wet one end and twirl it into a point. Thread it through one hole from the bottom.

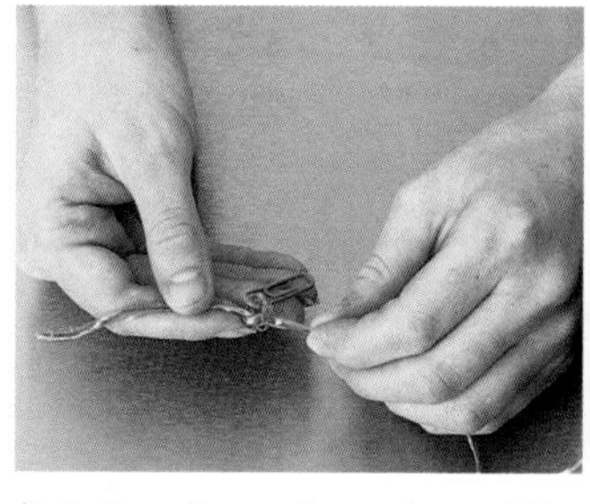

Pull the string through, and tie a paper clip to the end so it doesn't slip out of the hole. Do the same with the other cup.

If you let the string sag, the phone won't work.

Tell your friend to put one phone to his ear and walk away until the string is tight. Now speak—your voice makes the air in the cup vibrate, and the string starts to vibrate, too. The vibrations travel down the string, and at the other end, the cup vibrates and so does the air inside it. Your friend can hear what you're saying.

The smallest bones in your body are in your ears

## Rack and roll

Here's proof that sound travels better through solid things than through air.

Try "playing" other objects—different materials make different sounds.

Pull two coat hangers into diamond shapes. Hang an oven rack from the hooks, and hold the other ends while sticking your fingers in your ears. Now get a friend to "play" the rack with a spoon. Loud, isn't it? That's because sound waves go straight from solid metal to the solid bone of your head—and into your inner ears.

### High-sounding science

The closer together sound waves flow, the higher the sound (or pitch) they make. In the bottles below, the less air there is, the more the waves are squeezed together, and the higher the pitch. That's why the bottle with the most water gives the highest note.

Add a bit of food coloring for more colorful sounds.

## High five

Put different amounts of water in several bottles of the same size. Blow across the top of each one to make the air inside vibrate, then listen—which bottle gives the highest sound?

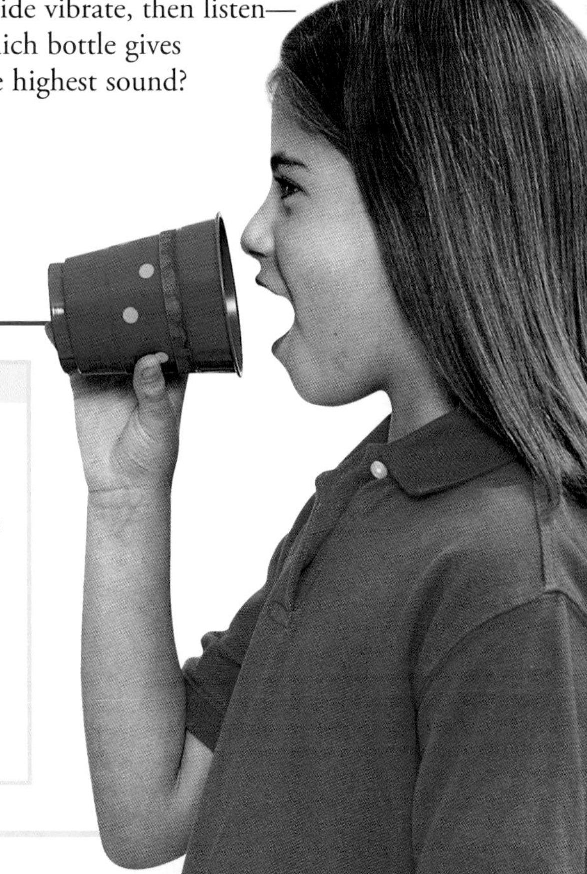

### Hearing science

When someone speaks to you, sound waves hit your ears and set your eardrums jiggling back and forth.This pushes on the tiniest bones of your body—those of the middle ear—and on the inner ear, too. There, cells tipped with tiny hairs turn the waves into nerve signals that zip off to your brain.

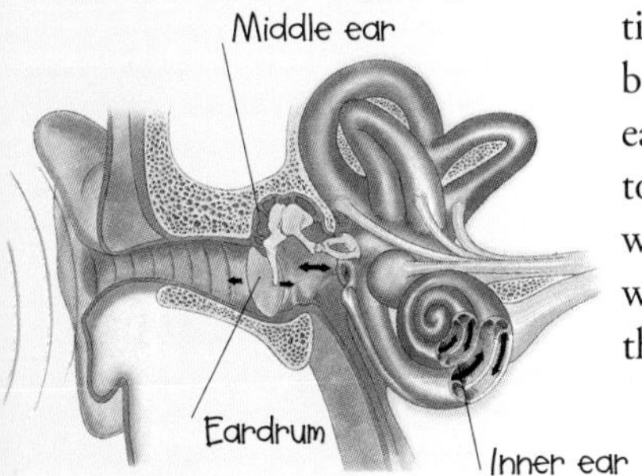

# Index

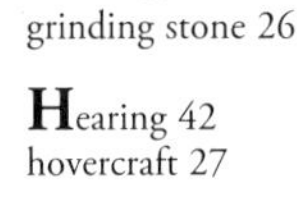

## Acknowledgments

**Chris Maynard** has written about 55 children's books. He won the Rhone-Poulenc Science Junior Book of the Year in 1996 (*The World of Weather*) and his *Informania Sharks* was runner up for the TES Senior Information Book Award in 1998. Recently, he has discovered the joys of writing websites, too.

**Dorling Kindersley would like to thank** the following people for their help in the production of this book: Trish Gant and Gary Ombler for additional photography, photographer's assistant Tracey Simmonds, Lara Tankel Holtz for the loan of her kitchen, Suzie Leaman for her help and understanding during the photo sessions, and the parents of all the budding scientists.

**Picture Credits**
The publisher would like to thank the following for their kind permission to reproduce their photographs:
(Key: a-above; b-below/bottom; c-center; f-far; l-left; r-right; t-top)
**Getty Images:** Iconica / Jamie Grill 43bc; The Image Bank / Nino Mascardi 32bc; Photodisc / Peter Gridley 45cr; Stone / Ezio Geneletti 32c; Stone /Frank Whitney 39crb; Taxi / Ivar Mjell 37cr.
**Science Photo Library:** Microfield Scientific Ltd 14br; Prof. P. Motta / Dept. Of Anatomy / University "La Sapienza", Rome 42cra; Peter Ryan 41cr. Binney Smith: 9cr.